W. T. Giffe

Glory Bells

A collection of new hymns and new music for Sunday-schools, gospel meetings,

revivals, Christian endeavor societies, Epworth leagues

W. T. Giffe

Glory Bells
A collection of new hymns and new music for Sunday-schools, gospel meetings, revivals, Christian endeavor societies, Epworth leagues

ISBN/EAN: 9783337083649

Printed in Europe, USA, Canada, Australia, Japan

Cover: Foto ©Lupo / pixelio.de

More available books at **www.hansebooks.com**

GLORY BELLS.

A COLLECTION OF

New Hymns and New Music

FOR

SUNDAY-SCHOOLS, GOSPEL MEETINGS, REVIVALS, CHRISTIAN ENDEAV-
OR SOCIETIES, EPWORTH
LEAGUES, ETC.

BY

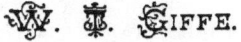
W. T. GIFFE.

Price, per doz. $3.60; per 100, $30. Single copy 35 cents.

PUBLISHED BY

THE HOME MUSIC CO.,
Logansport, Ind.

Copyright, 1896, by The Home Music Co.

Preface.

In making this book the author has aimed to have the hymns and music fresh and new throughout. With a very few exceptions, my purpose has been accomplished.

It will be seen that strong hands have helped in the contributions. Many more were placed at my disposal but not used, hence the public may feel sure that every number in this book is here by the most careful selection and because of its eminent merit and pleasing fitness for some useful place in the kingdom of religious song.

In order to secure the best efforts of the best composers, the publishers offered four cash prizes for the four best and most suitable contributions. These prizes were awarded by a committee of three persons, chosen because of their special qualifications in musical and literary knowledge, and long experience, viz: Mr. Chas. H. Gabriel, Dr. J. B. Herbert, and Mrs. Carre B. Adams.

It became necessary to divide the fourth prize between two pieces of supposed equal merit.

THIRTY-NINE COMPOSERS

competed for these prizes with ninty-one pieces. Besides the editor's own pieces, a number of others were barred from the competition for commercial reasons, etc.

All pieces entered for a prize are designated by (E. P.) printed at the lower right hand corner of the page. The pieces that won the prizes are indicated under the titles.

I hereby tender my grateful thanks to all who in any wise assisted in furnishing material and lessening the arduous task of making such a book, and this is meant also, for the many who submitted contributions, which, for lack of space, were necessarily omitted.

And now, asking God's blessing on its songs, we send forth GLORY BELLS to help sing a new wave of religious song throughout the land.

W. T. G.

WITH A SONG AND A PRAYER. Concluded.

WON'T YOU TRY, MY BROTHER? Concluded.

I WILL TRUST HIM. Concluded.

…

WELCOME THE ANGELS IN. Concluded.

BEAUTIFUL HOME, Concluded,

THERE IS WORK FOR YOU AND ME. Concluded.

33

Let Me Cling, O, Rock of Ages.

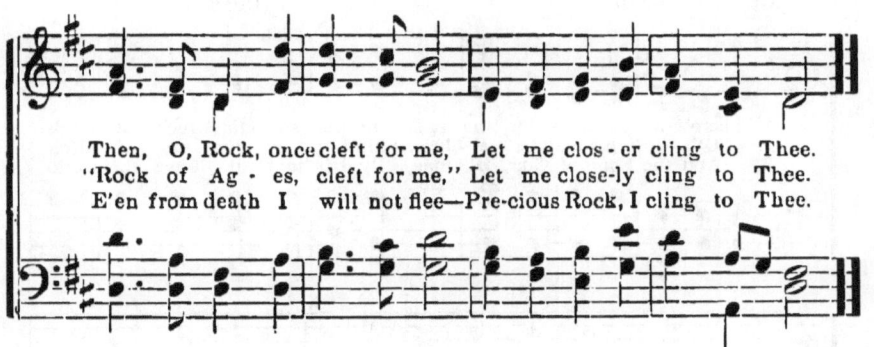

Then, O, Rock, once cleft for me, Let me clos-er cling to Thee.
"Rock of Ag - es, cleft for me," Let me close-ly cling to Thee.
E'en from death I will not flee—Pre-cious Rock, I cling to Thee.

No. 37.   OUR GLORIOUS HOME.

W. T. GIFFE.

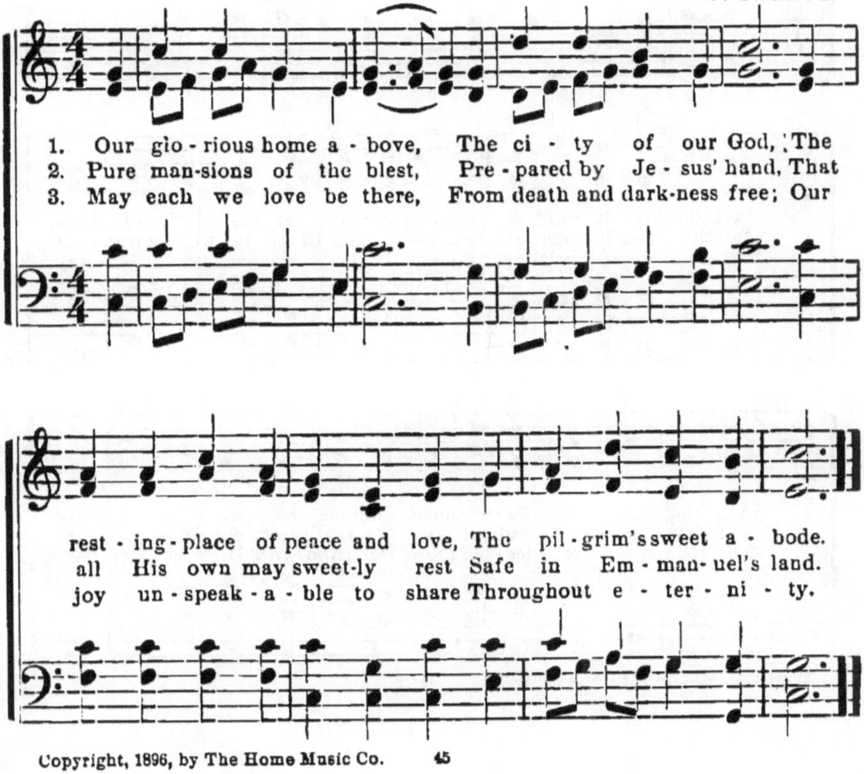

1. Our glo - rious home a - bove, The ci - ty of our God, The
2. Pure man-sions of the blest, Pre-pared by Je - sus' hand, That
3. May each we love be there, From death and dark-ness free; Our

rest - ing - place of peace and love, The pil - grim's sweet a - bode.
all His own may sweet-ly rest Safe in Em - man - uel's land.
joy un - speak - a - ble to share Throughout e - ter - ni - ty.

Copyright, 1896, by The Home Music Co.

God Knows.

CHORUS.

What mat-ter if the way be-yond Be - fore my gaze grow faint and dim?
God knows, I say! and am con-tent To trust it all to Him.

No. 52. CHILDREN'S DAY.

E. R. LATTA. W. T. G.

1. Why are fac - es all so cheer-y? Why are spir-its all so gay?
2. Why so man - y mer - ry voic - es, Join - ing in the gladsome lay?
3. Why so man - y fragrant blossoms, That their fair - y hues dis-play?

'Tis be-cause we here have gather'd, To ob-serve the Children's Day!
'Tis be-cause is fond - ly cherish'd, Each re-turn of Children's Day!
'Tis be-cause young hands have brought them, For the sake of Children's Day!

Copyright, 1896, by The Home Music Co.

Toiling in Life's Harvest.

No. 58.   BLEST BE THE TIE.

TUNE—Dennis. No. 29.

1 Blest be the tie that binds
  Our hearts in Christian love;
The fellowship of kindred minds
  Is like to that above.

2 Before our Father's throne,
  We pour our ardent prayers;
Our fears, our hopes, our aims are one—
  Our comforts and our cares.

3 We share our mutual woes;
  Our mutual burdens bear;
And often for each other flows
  The sympathizing tear.

4 When we asunder part,
  It gives us inward pain:
But we shall still be joined in heart,
  And hope to meet again.

Precious Love of Jesus.

No. 62. WHEN WE REACH THE HARBOR.

E. R. LATTA. O. L. FLECK.

1. When we reach the har - bor, Nev - er more to sail, Ours shall be the
2. When we reach the har - bor, And shall an-chor there, Freed from toil and
3. When we reach the har - bor On the Ca-naan side, Thro' the love and

pleas - ures That shall nev - er fail: Nev - er storm shall fright us,
dan - ger, Freed from sin and care! Oh, what hal - le - lu - jahs
mer - cy Of the Cru - ci - fied, Oh, how man - y dear ones

Ne'er a cloud shall frown, When with saints and angels We shall wear a crown.
From our lips shall rise! What a shout of tri-umph As we grasp the prize!
From that countless throng There will come to greet us, With a smile and song!

CHORUS.

Har - bor, O har - bor, peace - ful and bright, Free from all sor - row,

Copyright, 1896, by The Home Music Co.

Trusting in Jesus.

CHORUS.

I am trust-ing Thee, Lord Je-sus, I am trust-ing Thee to-day;
I am trust-ing in Thee on-ly, I will trust Thee all the way.

No. 65. A CHILD'S EVENING PRAYER.

W. T. G.   (Infant Class.)   W. T. GIFFE.

Andante.

1. Je-sus, wilt Thou guard the slum-ber Of a lit-tle child like me?
2. Yes, I know that Thou wilt keep me, So I close my wea-ry eyes,
3. In Thine arms, O Je-sus, fold me, Let me be Thy lit-tle lamb;

Wilt Thou watch in darkness o'er me, That pro-tect-ed I may be?
Pray-ing God to send His an-gels Down to guard me from the skies.
Close un-to Thy bo-som hold me; Give me slum-ber deep and calm.

Copyright, 1896, by The Home Music Co.

No. 70. O BETHLEHEM!

E. R. Latta. Geo. B. Holsinger.

1. O Beth-le-hem! thou cit-y blest, The in-fant Lord to hold;
2. O Beth-le-hem! in Ju-dah's land, On whom all eyes were cast;
3. O Beth-le-hem! we turn to Thee, By faith in Je-sus' name;

As 'twas in proph-e-cy expressed, In wondrous days of old!
Tho' small Thou art, Thy name shall stand As long as time shall last!
And tho' we ne'er Thy site may see, We love to sing Thy fame!

Tho' void of gran-deur be Thy walls, Thy streets appear for-lorn;
Such hon-ors as to thee be-long, Sur-pass all oth-ers far;
By faith we hear the strain to-day That o-ver thee was poured;

A voice from thee each Christmas calls, 'Twas here that Christ was born,
Im-man-u-el, the an-gel throng, And Ma-gi—Guid-ing Star!
By faith be-hold the won-drous ray That shone a-bove the Lord!

Copyright, 1896, by The Home Music Co.

No. 74. "HERE AM I."

"That the Lord called Samuel: and he answered, Here am I."—1st Sam. 3: 4.

Rev. T. C. SMITH.   A. F. MYERS.

Spirited.

1. As the Lord to Sam-uel spake, In si-lent night hours long gone by,
2. When the Lord calls you to strive A-gainst the wrongs that round you lie,
3. To the Sav-ior's gen-tle call, With meek and lov-ing heart re-ply,—
4. Christ a rich re-ward will give To you in His bright home on high,

If His voice should you a-wake, Would you an-swer Here am I?
Ev-'ry day of earth-ly life, Will you an-swer Here am I?
For Him free-ly leav-ing all, Glad-ly an-swer Here am I.
And He'll bless you while you live, If you'll an-swer Here am I.

CHORUS.

Here am I, Here am I, Here am I, Here am I, When my name is called I'll answer,

Here am I, Here am I, Here am I, Here am I, Here am I, Here am I,

Rit. Repeat Chorus pp.

When my name is called I'll an-swer, Here am I, Here am I.

Copyright, 1894, by A. F. Myers, Toledo, O. From "The Search Light." By per.

No. 76. I AM ETERNALLY FREE.

Rev. ELISHA A. HOFFMAN. H. M. BUTLER.

(Play the bass notes of the accompaniment in octaves.)

1. My Sa-vior was nailed to the cross,...... He bore my trans-gressions for me;...... He saved me from in-fi-nite loss,...... And I am e-ter-nal-ly free......
2. No dread con-dem-na-tion I fear,...... My per-fect Re-deemer is He;...... His words of for-give-ness I hear,......

3. My soul is a well-spring of praise,.... The Lord is so precious to me;...... All gladsome and

Copyright, 1896, by The Home Music Co.

I Am Eternally Free.

Shout, O Earth!

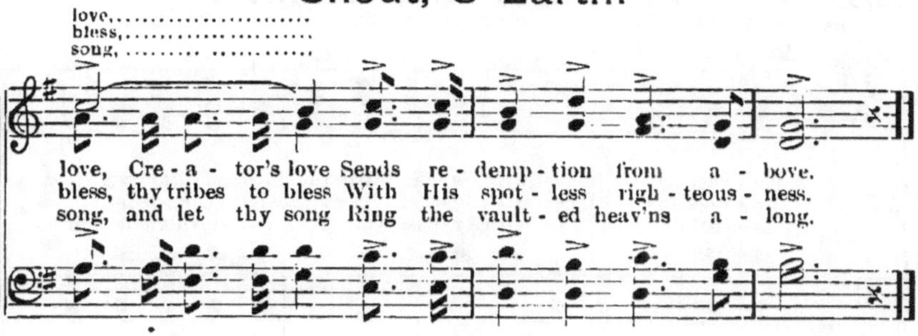

love, ...
bless, ...
song, ...

1. love, Crea-tor's love Sends re-demp-tion from a - bove.
2. bless, thy tribes to bless With His spot-less righ-teous-ness.
3. song, and let thy song Ring the vault-ed heav'ns a - long.

No. 96.   HE LEADETH ME.

W. T. GIFFE.

Andante.

1. 'Tis God's own hand that lead - eth me A - long life's pil-grim way;
2. 'Tis God's own hand that lead - eth me A - long my toil-some way;
3. 'Tis God's own hand that lead - eth me A - long my wea - ry way;
4. So God's own hand doth lead me on Thro' dark-ness and thro' gloom;

But not be - cause He need - eth me, I need Him for my stay.
And since in love He feed - eth me, I'll trust Him ev - 'ry day.
And ev - 'ry day He speed - eth me Tow'rd an e - ter - nal day.
And well I know wher - e'er I go His hand will lead me home.

CHORUS.

He lead - eth me, He lead - eth me, He lead - eth me.

Copyright, 1896, by The Home Music Co.

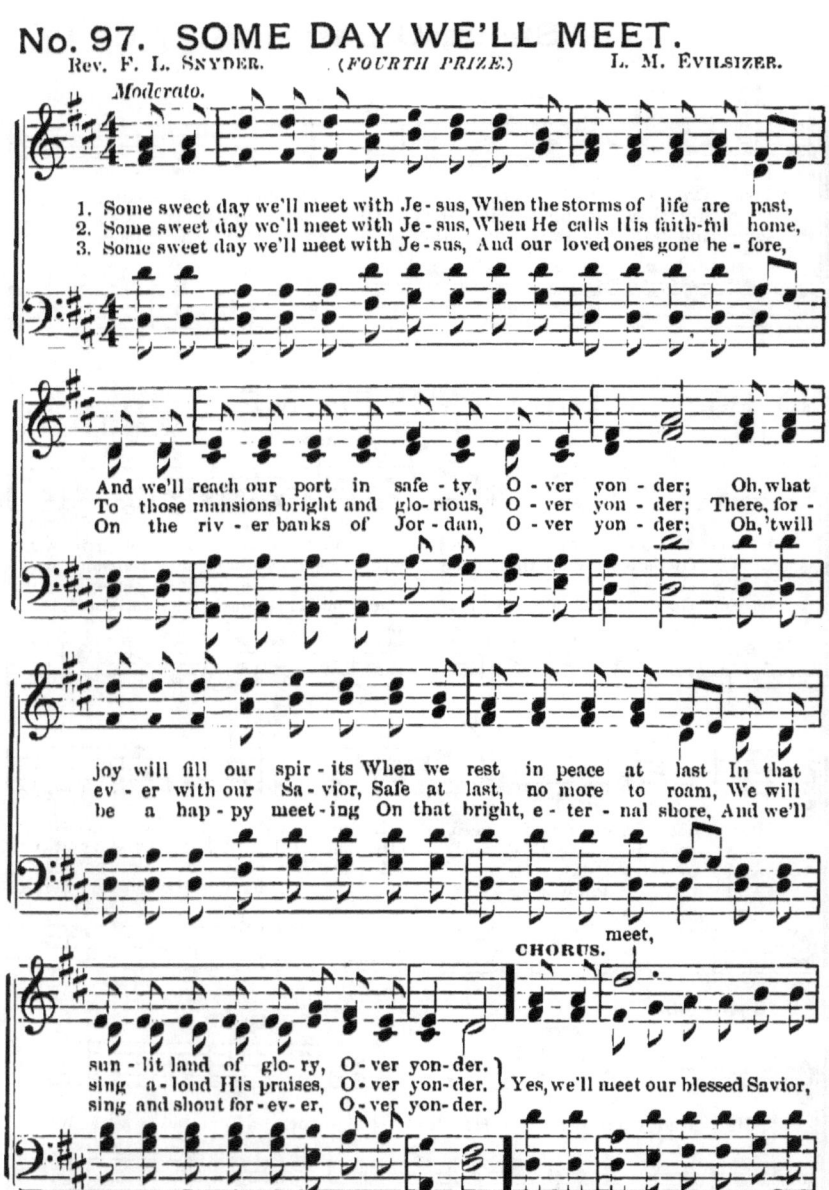

Some Day We'll Meet.

(Sheet music)

No. 98. MUST JESUS BEAR THE CROSS?

1 Must Jesus bear the cross alone,
And all the world go free?
No! there's a cross for every one,
And there's a cross for me.

2 The consecrated cross I'll bear,
Till death shall set me free,
And then go home my crown to wear,
For there's a crown for me.

3 O precious cross, O glorious crown!
O resurrection day!
Ye angels from the stars come down,
And bear my soul away.

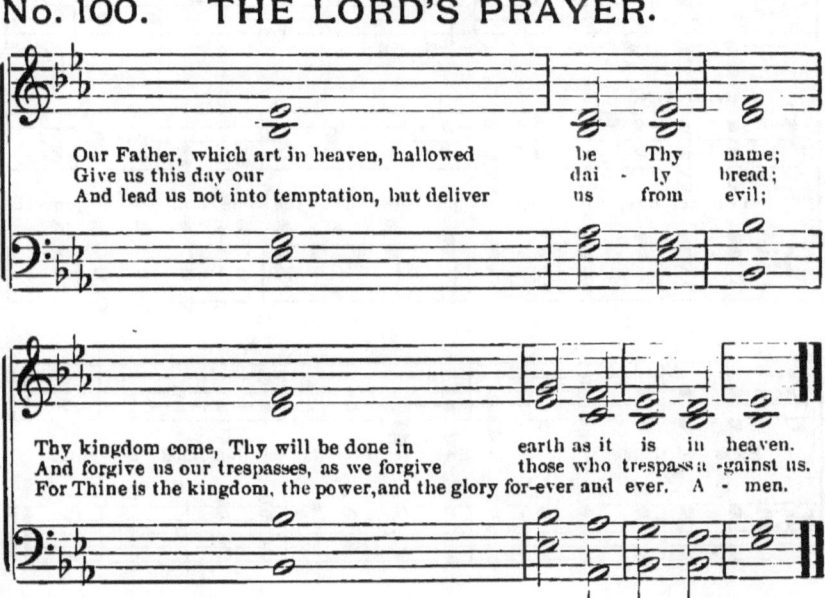

A SONG OF PRAISE.

good-ness and mer-cy we sing; He sought us in kind-ness, re-deemed us in love, And now we are heirs to His kingdom a-bove.

RESPONSIVE READINGS.

No. 1.

LEADER.—The heavens declare the glory of God, and the firmament showeth his handiwork.

RESPONSE.—Day unto day uttereth speech, and night unto night showeth knowledge.

L.—The law of the Lord is perfect, converting the soul.

R.—The testimony of the Lord is sure, making wise the simple.

L.—The statutes of the Lord are right, rejoicing the heart.

R.—The commandment of the Lord is pure, enlightening the eyes.

L.—The fear of the Lord is clean, enduring forever.

R.—The judgments of the Lord are true, and righteous altogether.

No. 2.

LEADER.—Bless the Lord, O my soul; and all that is within me, bless his holy name.

RESPONSE.—Bless the Lord, O my soul, and forget not all his benefits:

L.—Who forgiveth all thine iniquities: who healeth all thy diseases;

R.—Who redeemeth thy life from destruction: who crowneth thee with loving kindness and tender mercies:

L.—Who satisfieth thy mouth with good things: so that thy youth is renewed like the eagles.

R.—He hath not dealt with us after our sins: nor rewarded us according to our iniquities.

L.—For as the heaven is high above the earth, so great is his mercy toward them that fear him.

R.—As far as the east is from the west, so far hath he removed our transgressions from us.

MARCHING TO GLORY.

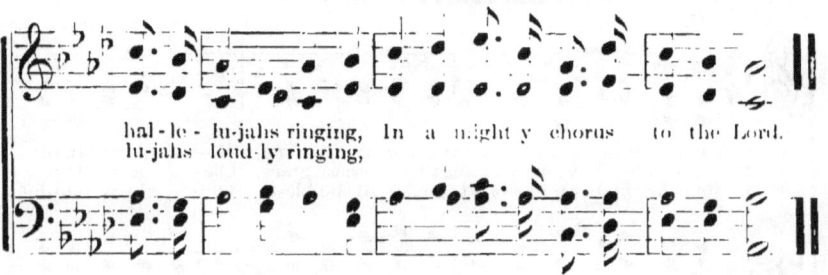

hal-le-lu-jahs ringing, In a mighty chorus to the Lord.
lu-jahs loudly ringing,

No. 105. COME, THE SAVIOUR CALLETH.

IDA REED. W. T. GIFFE.

1. Come, the Saviour call-eth, Come, my child to me; Low the accents
2. Come, He still is pleading, In my arms find rest; By my love I'll
3. Come, He crieth, fear not, Un-to Je-sus go; Tell Him all thy

CHORUS.

fall-eth, I will com-fort thee.
lead thee, Still thy troubled breast. Come, the Sav-iour call-eth,
tri-als, If thou peace would know.

p *pp*

Bring to me thy care; Low the sweet words falleth, I thy griefs will bear.

Copyright, 1896, by The Home Music Co.

117

CHILDREN'S DAY SONG.

The beau - ti - ful blossoms That cheer us tho' dreary the day.
The beautiful, delicate blossoms, sweet blossoms,

No. 109. CORONATION.

PERONET.   OLIVER HOLDEN.

1. All hail the pow'r of Je - sus' name, Let an-gels prostrate fall;
2. Let ev-'ry kin-dred, ev - 'ry tribe, On this ter - res-trial ball,
3. Oh, that with yon-der sa-cred throng, We at His feet may fall;

Bring forth the roy-al di - a-dem, And crown Him Lord of all;
To Him all maj - es - ty ascribe, And crown Him Lord of all;
We'll join the ev - er - last-ing song, And crown Him Lord of all;

Bring forth the roy-al di - a-dem, And crown Him Lord of all.
To Him all maj - es - ty ascribe, And crown Him Lord of all.
We'll join the ev - er - lasting song, And crown Him Lord of all.

THE BELLS OF TIME.

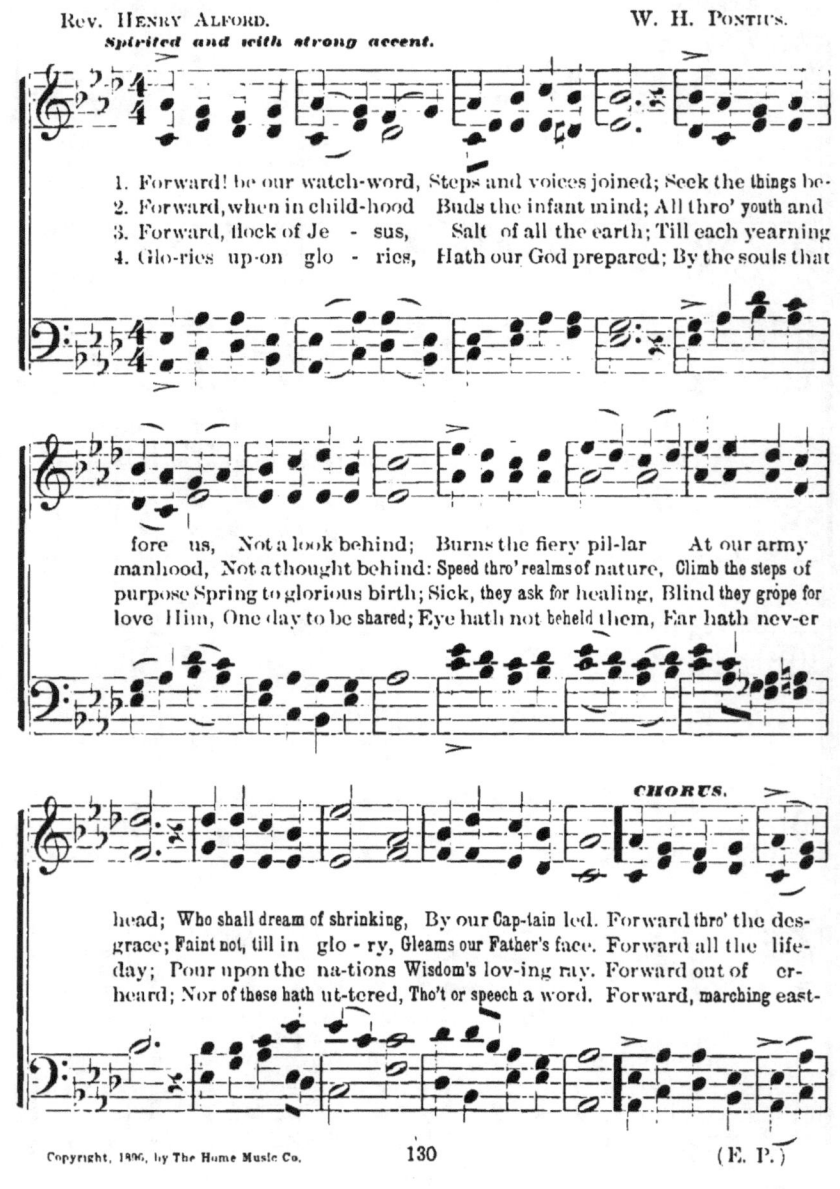

No. 117. FORWARD! BE OUR WATCHWORD.

Rev. HENRY ALFORD.   W. H. PONTIUS.

Spirited and with strong accent.

1. Forward! be our watch-word, Steps and voices joined; Seek the things be-
2. Forward, when in child-hood Buds the infant mind; All thro' youth and
3. Forward, flock of Je - sus, Salt of all the earth; Till each yearning
4. Glo-ries up-on glo - ries, Hath our God prepared; By the souls that

fore us, Not a look behind; Burns the fiery pil-lar At our army
manhood, Not a thought behind: Speed thro' realms of nature, Climb the steps of
purpose Spring to glorious birth; Sick, they ask for healing, Blind they grope for
love Him, One day to be shared; Eye hath not beheld them, Ear hath nev-er

CHORUS.

head; Who shall dream of shrinking, By our Cap-tain led. Forward thro' the des-
grace; Faint not, till in glo - ry, Gleams our Father's face. Forward all the life-
day; Pour upon the na-tions Wisdom's lov-ing ray. Forward out of er-
heard; Nor of these hath ut-tered, Tho't or speech a word. Forward, marching east-

Copyright, 1896, by The Home Music Co.   (E. P.)

FORWARD! BE OUR WATCHWORD.

ert, Thro' the toil and fight; Jordan flows before us, Zion beams with light.
time, Climb from height to height; Till the head be hoary, Till the eye be light.
ror, Leave behind the night; Forward thro' the darkness, Forward into light.
ward Where the beam is bright; Till the vale be lifted, Till our faith be sight.

No. 118.   PRAISES TO OUR KING.

Rev. GODFREY THRING.   INFANT CLASS.   HENRY A. LEWIS.

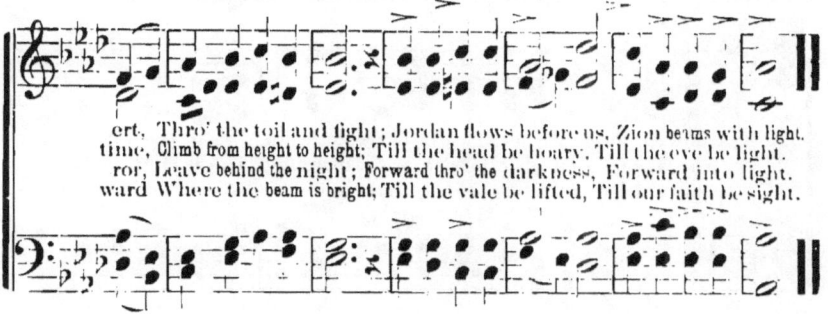

1. Saviour, blessed Saviour, Listen while we sing; Hearts and voices raising
2. Great and ever greater, Are Thy mercies here; True and ever lasting,

Praises to our King, All we have to offer, All we hope to be; Body, soul and spirit, All we yield to Thee.
Are the glories there, Where no pain or sorrow, Toil or care are known; When the angel legions, Circle round Thy throne.

Copyright, 1896, by The Home Music Co.

ONWARD, FOREVER.

faith - ful - ly, ev - er, Vic-tors thro' Him all who strive shall be.

No. 120. TO PLEASE THE KING.

INFANT CLASS.   HENRY A. LEWIS.

1. Oh, what can lit - tle hands do, To please the King of heav'n? The
2. Oh, what can lit - tle lips do, To please the King of heav'n? The
3. Oh, what can lit - tle eyes do, To please the King of heav'n? The
4. Oh, what can lit - tle hearts do, To please the King of heav'n? The

lit - tle hands some work may try That will some sim - ple
lit - tle lips can praise and pray, And gen - tle words of
lit - tle eyes can up - ward look, And learn to read God's
hearts, if He His Spir - it send, Can love Him, Mak - er,

want sup-ply, Such grace to mine be giv'n, Such grace to mine be giv'n.
kind-ness say, Such grace to mine be giv'n, Such grace to mine be giv'n.
ho - ly book, Such grace to mine be giv'n, Such grace to mine be giv'n.
Saviour, Friend, Such grace to mine be giv'n, Such grace to mine be giv'n.

Copyright 1896 by The Home Music Co.

RAISE THE SIGNAL.

No. 122. THE CHILDREN'S HYMN.
INFANT CLASS.
W. T. G.

1. Lord, a lit-tle band and low-ly, We are come to worship Thee;
2. Fill our hearts with tho'ts of Je-sus, And of heav'n where He is gone;
3. For we know the Lord of glo-ry, Al-ways sees what children do;

Thou art great, and high and ho-ly, Oh, how humble we should be.
And let noth-ing ev-er please us, He would grieve to look up-on.
Ev-en now He knows the sto-ry, Of our tho'ts and actions too.

Copyright, 1896, by The Home Music Co.

No. 125. JUNIOR LEAGUE MARCH.

LAURA E. NEWELL. CHAS. K. LANGLEY.

May be used as a march song.

1. We're a hap-py, happy band, Marching to the promised land! In our
2. We are weak, but He is strong, Jesus is our strength and song; Little
3. Je-sus calls us to the fold, Ere our hearts grow hard and cold; Come and

CHORUS.

Junior League rejoice—Worship Je-sus, heart and voice. Je-sus loves us,
pilgrims! still we sing Hal - le - lu - jah, to our King!
join our youthful band, Marching to Immanuel's land. Je-sus loves

ev - 'ry day, Leads us in the nar-row way;
us ev - ry day, Leads us in the nar-row way;

We will praise Him day and night, Praise Him for His gos-pel light.

Copyright, 1896, by The Home Music Co.

No. 127. WORKING FOR THE MASTER.

IDA S. LEWIS.   CHRISTIAN ENDEAVOR SONG.   HENRY A. LEWIS.

1. Work-ing for the Mas-ter, With a pur-pose true,   Be a will-ing
2. Speak a word of com-fort To the soul dis-tressed, Teach the words of
3. Oft-en words of kindness, If we on-ly knew, Break the clouds of

help-er In all you find to do;   Try to lead the err-ing
Je-sus, "I will give you rest;"   Do not be dis-cour-aged,
dark-ness, Let-ting sunshine through; Wea-ry not, but la-bor,

From the paths of sin,   To the blessed ha-ven, Bid them enter in.
Tho' they do not heed,   He will surely smile on Ev'ry lov-ing deed.
'Till your work is done, And you hear the welcome, "Child of love, come home."

CHORUS.

Work - ing for Je - sus, With a pur - pose true,
Working, yes, working for Je - sus, With a pur-pose, a purpose so true,

Copyright, 1896, by The Home Music Co.   (E. P.)

WORKING FOR THE MASTER.

Loy-al be and faith-ful All life's journey thro', All life's jour-ney thro'.

No. 128. LAMBS OF THE FLOCK.

INFANT CLASS.   W. G. Thomas.

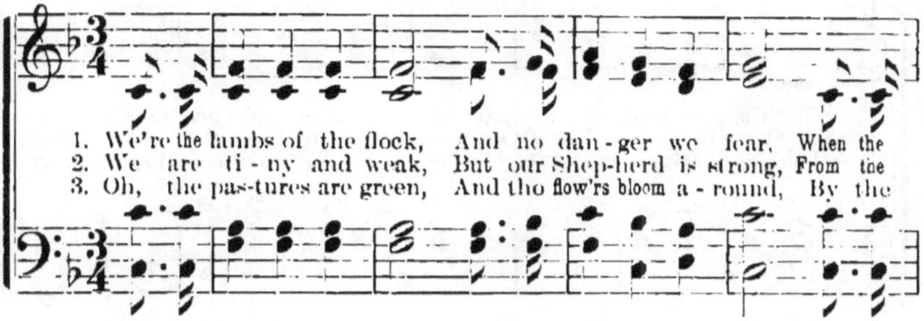

1. We're the lambs of the flock, And no dan-ger we fear, When the
2. We are ti-ny and weak, But our Shep-herd is strong, From the
3. Oh, the pas-tures are green, And the flow'rs bloom a-round, By the

voice and the call   Of our Shepherd we hear.
wolves He'll defend,   Keep us all the day long.
wa-ters so still,   Je-sus lets us lie down.

CHORUS.

We will follow, yes, we'll follow, We will follow His call, When our Shepherd we hear, We will follow His call.

Copyright, by W. T. Giffe.

No. 129. THE PALACE IN THE VALE.

W. A. Ogden, by per. SUITABLE FOR FUNERALS. W. T. Giffe.

1. One by one the loving Master Bid His tired reapers come
2. One by one they drop their sickles, Tho' the harvest fields are white;
3. One by one they join the chorus, Of the blessed ones above,

To the glad feast of rejoicing, In the palace halls of home.
They have heard the Master's summons, Wafted from the halls of light.
Tuning heart and voice together, In the mighty song of love.

REFRAIN.

One by one, yes, one by one, Earthly life and vision fail,

Then upon our raptured sight Bursts the palace in the vale.

Copyright, by W T Giffe.

No. 134. I AM COMING TO THEE.

Rev. Elisha A. Hoffman.   W. T. Giffe.

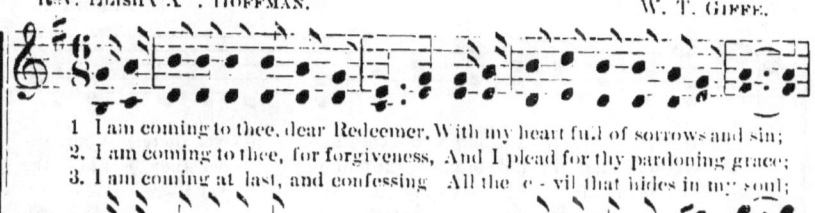

1. I am coming to thee, dear Redeemer, With my heart full of sorrows and sin;
2. I am coming to thee, for forgiveness, And I plead for thy pardoning grace;
3. I am coming at last, and confessing All the e - vil that hides in my soul;

And I pray thee in tender compassion, In my soul thy sal-va-tion be - gin.
All my many and shameful transgressions From thy book of remembrance efface.
And I plead for thy grace and thy blessing, And I pray thee, Dear Lord, make me whole.

CHORUS.

I'm com-ing, dear Jesus, I'm com ing to thee, I'm coming with all my sin;

This moment I pray thee for - give me And the work of salvation be - gin.

Copyright, 1896, by The Home Music Co.

Unto Thee Will I Sing.

Lord, who in mer-cy so free Hath crowned with love all my days.

No. 138. DOUBT NOT GOD'S GOOD PURPOSE.

E. S. D.
Moderato.

Emma S. Day
Arr. by W. T. G.

1. Doubt not God's good purpose; In His will be strong, Tho' thy way be
2. Wav-er not, tho' tempted; Mur-mur not, tho' tried; Be con-tent to
3. Let not mys-tic shad-ows Rob thy faith of sight; Yield not to their

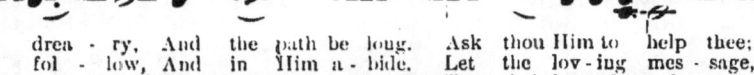

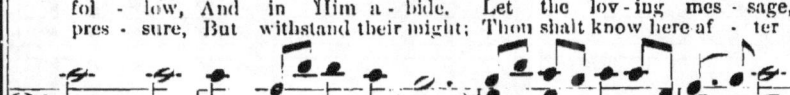

drea - ry, And the path be long. Ask thou Him to help thee;
fol - low, And in Him a - bide. Let the lov-ing mes - sage,
pres - sure, But withstand their might; Thou shalt know here af - ter

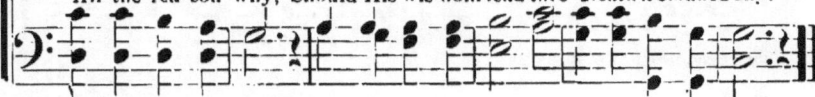

Trust in Him to lead; Thou wilt find Him careful Of thy smallest need.
"Hold fast till I come," Re - en-force thy courage, All the jour-ney home.
All the rea-son why, Should His wis-dom lead thee 'Neath a clouded sky.

Copyright, 1896, by The Home Music Co.

We'll Overthrow the Wrong.

Come, Oh, Come to Me!

No. 147. THE LORD IS MY REFUGE.

R. A. Evilsizer. J. A. Smith.

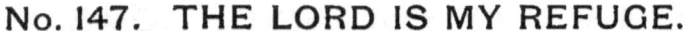

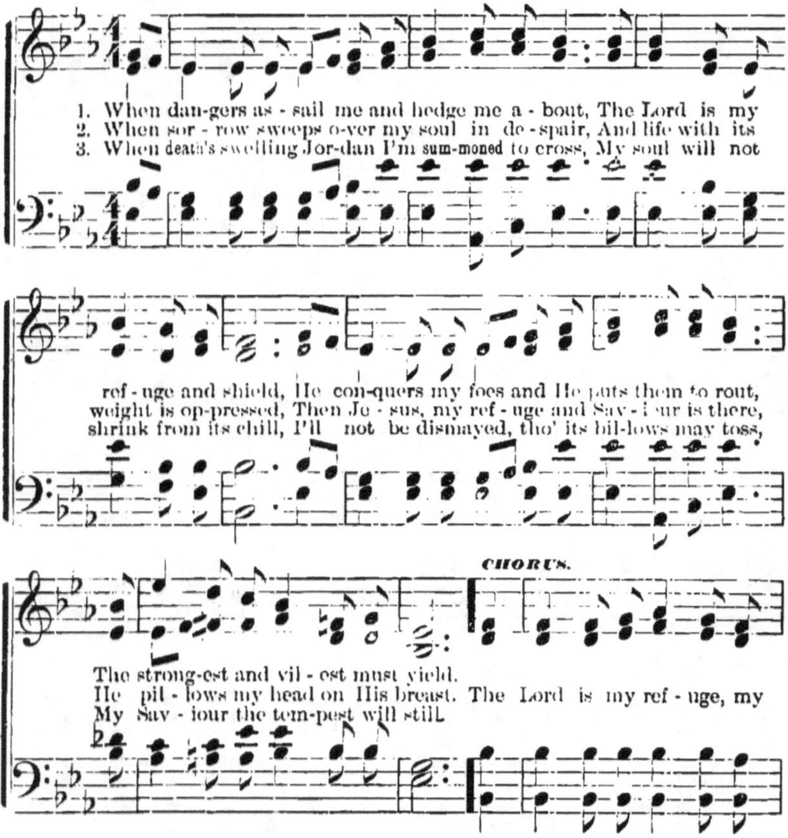

(E. P.)

No. 149. WE ARE LITTLE TOILERS.

IDA L. REED.   PRIMARY CLASS.   R. A. GLEEN.

1. We are lit-tle toil-ers, For our Lord and King, Pa-tient-ly we
2. We are lit-tle toil-ers, In His vine-yard fair, We with joy are
3. We are lit-tle toil-ers, Day by day we bring Un-to Christ our

labor, Love's sweet gifts to bring, Unto Him who loves us, Humble tho' they be,
filling Our small places there, Jesus helps us onward, All our ways doth see,
Saviour, Some sweet offering, He doth bless our toiling, Gladdens all our way

CHORUS.

Yet our Lord will bless them, In His mer-cy free. We are lit-tle
Will-ing lit-tle servants, Un-to Him we'll be.
And for Him we'll ev-er La-bor day by day. We are lit-tle

toil - - ers,   For   our Lord and King,
toil-ers, lit-tle toil-ers, For our Lord, our Lord and King,

Copyright, 1896, by The Home Music Co.   164   (E. P.

GO FORTH, YE BRAVE ENDEAVORERS!

THE BRIGHT FOR EVERMORE.

mong the fair, In the bright for ev - er - more.
mong the fair, a-mong the fair, In the bright for ev-ermore, ev-er - more.

No. 157. The Reaper and the Flowers.
FOR FUNERALS.

Henry W. Longflelow.   W. T. Giffe.

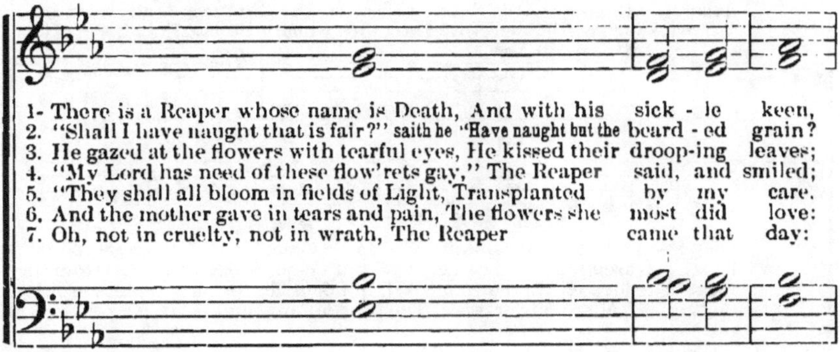

1- There is a Reaper whose name is Death, And with his sick - le keen,
2. "Shall I have naught that is fair?" saith he "Have naught but the beard - ed grain?
3. He gazed at the flowers with tearful eyes, He kissed their droop-ing leaves;
4. "My Lord has need of these flow'rets gay," The Reaper said, and smiled;
5. "They shall all bloom in fields of Light, Transplanted by my care.
6. And the mother gave in tears and pain, The flowers she most did love:
7. Oh, not in cruelty, not in wrath, The Reaper came that day:

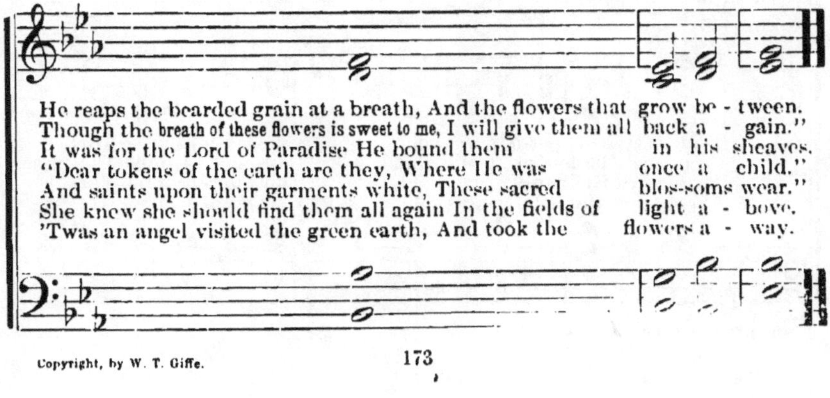

He reaps the bearded grain at a breath, And the flowers that grow be - tween.
Though the breath of these flowers is sweet to me, I will give them all back a - gain."
It was for the Lord of Paradise He bound them in his sheaves.
"Dear tokens of the earth are they, Where He was once a child."
And saints upon their garments white, These sacred blos-soms wear."
She knew she should find them all again In the fields of light a - bove.
'Twas an angel visited the green earth, And took the flowers a - way.

Copyright, by W. T. Giffe.

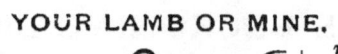

YOUR LAMB OR MINE.

gane fra the fold? Is it your lamb or mine That is gane fra the fold?
far from the fold? Is it your lamb or mine That's sae far from the fold?
gane fra the fold, Be it your lamb or mine That is gane fra the fold.
turns to the fold? Is it your lamb or mine He returns to the fold?

No. 159. HOLY, LORD GOD ALMIGHTY.

R. HEBER, D. D. Rev. J. B. DYKES.

1. Ho-ly, Ho-ly, Ho - ly! Lord God Al-might-y! Ear-ly in the
2. Ho-ly, Ho-ly, Ho - ly! All the saints adore Thee, Casting down their
3. Ho-ly, Ho-ly, Ho - ly! Tho' the darkness hide Thee, Tho' the eyes of

morn - ing our songs shall rise to Thee; Ho-ly, Ho-ly Ho - ly!
golden crowns around the glass-y sea; Cher-u-bim and Sera-phim
sin-ful man Thy glo-ry may not see; On-ly Thou art ho - ly.

Mer-ci-ful and Might-y! God in three per-sons, blessed Trin-i-ty!
fall-ing down before Thee, Which wert and art, and ev-ermore shalt be.
there is none beside Thee, Per-fect in pow'r, in love and pur-i-ty.

Why Stand Ye Here Idle?—Concluded.

No. 163. THE PLACE I LOVE.

W. T. G.   (Infant Class.)   W. T. GIFFE.

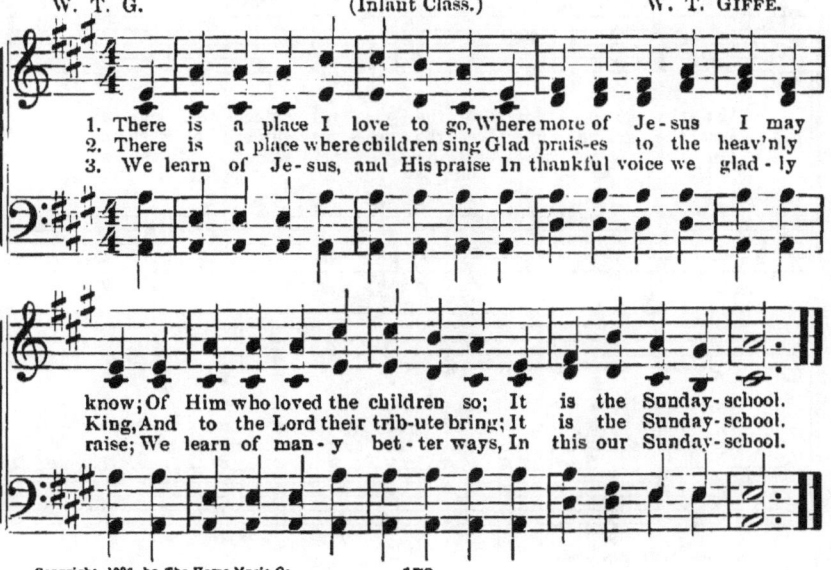

Copyright, 1896, by The Home Music Co.

Let the Gospel Shine.

pow'r to save and keep you, prove, Oh, let the gos-pel shine.
hap-py heart and cheer-ful face, You'll let the gos-pel shine.
then what bliss 'twill be to know You let the gos-pel shine.

CHORUS. Vigorously.

Let the gos-pel shine, Let the gos-pel shine; Je-sus, fill this heart of mine, And help me, oh, help me to let the gos-pel shine.

No. 165. RESPONSIVE READING.

LEADER.—The grass withereth, the flower fadeth; but the word of our God shall stand forever.

RESPONSE.—Hast thou not known? hast thou not heard,

L. That the everlasting God, the Lord, the Creator of the ends of the earth,

R. Fainteth not, neither is weary? there is no searching of his understanding.

L. He giveth power to the faint;

R. And to them that have no might he increaseth strength.

L. Even the youths shall faint and be weary,

R. And the young men shall utterly fall;

L. But they that wait upon the Lord shall renew their strength;

R. They shall mount up with wings as eagles;

L. They shall run, and not be weary: and they shall walk, and not faint.

Soldiers of the Lord.

Just The Same To-day.

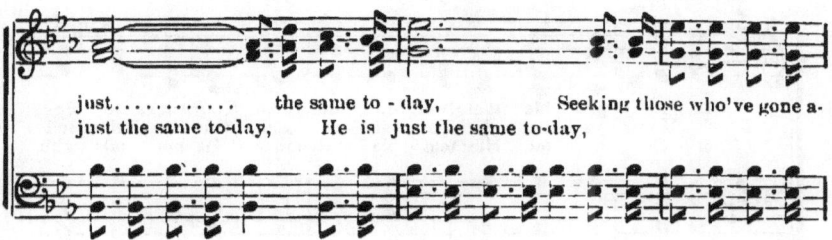

just............ the same to - day, Seeking those who've gone a-
just the same to-day, He is just the same to-day,
stray, Sav - ing souls a-long the way, Thank God! He's just the same to - day.

No. 172. BETHANY.

1 Nearer, my God, to Thee,
    Nearer to Thee!
E'en though it be a cross
    That raiseth me;
Still all my song shall be,
Nearer, my God, to Thee,
    Nearer to thee.

2 Though, like the wanderer,
    The sun gone down,
Darkness be over me,
    My rest a stone;
Yet in my dreams I'd be
Nearer, my God, to Thee,
    Nearer to Thee.

3 There let the way appear
    Steps unto heaven;
All that Thou sendest me,
    In mercy given;

Angels to beckon me
Nearer, my God, to Thee,
    Nearer to Thee.

4 Then with my waking thoughts
    Bright with Thy praise,
Out of my stony grief
    Bethel I'll raise;
So by my woes to be
Nearer, my God, to Thee,
    Nearer to Thee.

5 Or if on joyful wing
    Cleaving the sky,
Sun, moon, and stars forgot,
    Upward I fly,
Still all my song shall be,
Nearer, my God, to Thee,
    Nearer to Thee.

Vith Thankful Acclaim.

mer-cy to us nev-er ends, (nev-er ends); His faith-ful-ness true to His word, (to His word), Thro' a-ges un-end-ing ex-tends.

No. 174. RESPONSIVE READING.

LEADER.—For God so loved the world that He gave His only begotten Son, that whosoever believeth in Him should not perish, but have everlasting life.

RESPONSE.—I am the resurrection and the life: he that believeth in me, though he were dead, yet shall he live: and whosoever liveth and believeth in me shall never die.

L.—He maketh His wind to blow and the waters flow.

R.—The vine shall give her fruit, and the ground shall give her increase, and the heavens shall give their dew.

L.—Honor the Lord with thy substance, and with the first fruits of all thine increase.

R.—Give unto the Lord the glory due His name; bring an offering and come before Him.

L.—Bring ye all the tithes into the store-house, * * * and prove me now, saith the Lord of hosts, if I will not open you the windows of heaven, and pour you out a blessing, that there shall not be room enough to receive it.

R.—Of all that Thou shalt give me, I will surely give the tenth unto Thee.

L.—Not grudgingly, or of necessity, for God loveth a cheerful giver.

R.—Freely ye have received, freely give.

L.—My son, give me thine heart.

R.—Thy face, Lord, will I seek.

No. 179. SHALL I BE WORTHY.

E. R. Latta. W. T. Giffe.

1. When Jesus gathers His children, From all directions, in,
2. When Jesus gathers His children, Of ev-'ry age and name,
3. When Jesus gathers His children, With tones and looks of love.

Who've chosen Him for their Master, And He has cleansed from sin;
And welcomes them to His kingdom, Because they o-ver-came;
And they, thro' beautiful portals, Shall pass to bliss above;

The morn of the resurrection, In ev-'ry earth-ly zone;
Shall I be ready to answer The call of Christ, my Lord,
Shall you be one of the number, Who, faithful here have been,

Shall I be one of the number, He reckons as His own?
And share, for-ev-er and ev-er, The Christian's blest re-ward?
And go no more out, for-ev-er, To suf-fer or to sin?

Copyright, 1896, by The Home Music Co.

No. 181. UNDER HIS BANNER.

LAURA E. NEWELL.   W. H. BURGETT.

1. Under His banner we march to-day, Loy-al-ly forward we go!
2. Under His banner we'll do His will, Do as He'd have us to do
3. Under His banner we'll live and die, Heedless of toil or of pain,

Je-sus, our Captain, doth lead the way, Will we His or-ders know.
Heart-i-ly striv-ing to well ful-fill, Tasks, with the end in view.
Striv-ing for mansions prepared on high, Where we with Christ shall reign.

Onward, press onward, and turn not back; You would unworthy prove,
Onward, tho' en-e-mies stern-ly frown; Knowing His smile, we'll see,
Firm in His ranks are we marching home, Soon with the conflict done.

If you retreat, you would courage lack, Follow the God you love.
Soon we shall lay all the ar-mor down, Joyous in vic-to-ry.
We shall re-joice at the summons, Come, When we the crown have won.

Copyright, 1896, by The Home Music Co.

Bringing Back the Wanderers.

CHORUS.

Oh, who will go........ and seek to day, ... The wand'ring
Oh, who will go, and seek to-day,

ones..... who've gone astray?..... Go tell the sto - - - - - ry sweet and
The wand'ring ones who've gone astray? Go tell the story sweet and

old,........ And bring them to............ the Sav-ior's fold.
old, sweet and old, And bring them to the Sav-ior's fold

No. 186. RESPONSIVE READING.

MATT. 5:12.

1. And seeing the multitude, He went up into a mountain: and when He was set, His disciples came unto Him:

2. And He opened His mouth and taught them, saying,

3. Blessed are the poor in spirit: for theirs is the kingdom of heaven.

4. Blessed are they that mourn: for they shall be comforted.

5. Blessed are the meek: for they shall inherit the earth.

6. Blessed are they which do hunger and thirst after righteousness: for they shall be filled.

7. Blessed are the merciful: for they shall obtain mercy.

8. Blessed are the pure in heart: for they shall see God.

9. Blessed are the peacemakers: for they shall be called the children of God.

10. Blessed are they which are persecuted for righteousness' sake: for theirs is the kingdom of heaven.

11. Blessed are ye when men shall revile you, and persecute you, and shall say all manner of evil against you falsely for my sake.

12. Rejoice, and be exceeding glad: for great is your reward in heaven: for so persecuted they the prophets which were before you.

His Love is Just the Same.

No. 188. RESPONSIVE READING.

Psa. 96.

1. O sing unto the Lord a new song; sing unto the Lord all the earth.

2. Sing unto the Lord, bless His name; show forth His salvation from day to day.

3. Declare His glory among the heathen His wonders among all people.

4. For the Lord is great, and greatly to be praised: He is to be feared above all Gods.

5. For all the gods of the nations are idols: but the Lord made the heavens.

6. Honor and majesty are before Him. Strength and beauty are in His sanctuary.

7. Give unto the Lord, O ye kindreds of the people, give unto the Lord glory and strength.

8. Give unto the Lord the glory due unto His name: bring an offering and come into His courts.

9. O worship the Lord in the beauty of holiness: fear before Him, all the earth.

10. Say among the heathen that the Lord reigneth: the world also shall be established that it shall not be moved. He shall judge the people righteously.

11. Let the heavens rejoice, and let the earth be glad: let the sea roar and the fullness thereof.

12. Let the field be joyful and all that is therein: then shall all the trees of the wood rejoice.

13. Before the Lord: for He cometh, for He cometh to judge the earth: He shall judge the world with righteousness, and the people with His truth.

INDEX.

Titles in Small Capitals. First Lines in Roman Letters.

Title	No.	Title	No.
AMERICA	10	CROWNING BY AND BY, (The)	111
AT THE CROSS	13	COME IN, COME IN	113
AT THE BEAUTIFUL GATE	32	Come, Ye Blessed of My Father	94
ALL THE WORLD IS PRAISING HIM	34	CHRIST IS CHIEF IN HEAVEN	79
AVON	27	CHILD'S EVENING PRAYER	65
A LITTLE CHILD	31	Come, Oh, Come to Me	144
ALL THROUGH THE NIGHT	148		
All Hail the Power of Jesus' Name	109	DENNIS	29
A SONG OF PRAISE	103	DOUBT NOT GOD'S GOOD PURPOSE	138
A THOUSAND YEARS	88	DOOR OF THE KINGDOM	107
ABIDE WITH ME	78	EVENTIDE	78
A CHILD'S EVENING PRAYER	65	EVERY ONE THAT THIRSTETH	60
A LAST PRAYER	61		
AT THE SAVIOR'S RIGHT HAND	175	Forever Here my Rest Shall Be	27
		FROM EARTH TO HEAVEN	48
BEAUTIFUL HOME	22	Forward! Be our Watchword	117
BELIEVER'S HOPE, (The)	47		
BRINGING BACK THE WANDERERS	185	God Never is Tired of Forgiving	9
BEAUTIFUL HOME OVER THERE	135	GLORY TO THE LAMB	11
BECKONING LIGHT, (The)	160	GLORIA PATRI	17
BRIGHT FOREVERMORE, (The)	156	Glory be to the Father	17
BY AND BY WILL COME THE MORN	154	GATHER THE GOLDEN GRAIN	33
BELLS OF TIME	110	GOD KNOWS	51
BRING THEM INTO THE FOLD	85	GLORY BELLS	1
BLEST BE THE TIE	58	GOD OF THE NATIONS	39
BE A SOLDIER OF THE CROSS	56	GOD BLESS THE LITTLE ONES	130
BEAUTIFUL LIGHTS OF HOME	141	GO FORTH, YE BRAVE ENDEAVORER	151
BRING THEM IN	183	Golden Somewhere, (The)	155
BANNER OF THE CROSS, (The)	28	GOD IS LOVE	101
BETHANY	172	GLORIA PATRI	90
CLEANSING BLOOD, (The)	12	How Gentle God's Commands	28
CHILDREN'S DAY	52	HAPPY AS WE LABOR	42
CARTWRIGHT	140	HIS SATISFYING LOVE	26
COME TO HIS LOVING ARMS	152	HOLY LORD GOD ALMIGHTY	159
CHILDREN'S DAY SONG	108	HE IS CALLING THEE	114
CORONATION	109	HE LEADETH ME	96
COME, THE SAVIOR CALLETH	105	HAPPY, HAPPY, HAPPY	83
CHILDREN OF A KING	106	HERE AM I	74
CHILDREN'S HYMN	122	Ho! Every One that Thirsteth	60
COMING OF THE KING, (The)	112	HIS LOVE IS JUST THE SAME	187

(206)

INDEX.

Title	No.	Title	No.
IN THE GOLDEN BY AND BY	166	NEVER TIRED OF FORGIVING	9
I WILL TRUST HIM	8	NEATH THE BANNER OF THE CROSS	28
I Will Trust the Lord Forever	8	NEITHER DO I CONDEMN THEE	46
I Hear my Savior Calling	19	Nearer, My God, to Thee	172
In this World so Full of Sadness	25		
I would Bathe in the Fountain	30	O HAPPY DAY	6
I Think I should Mourn	32	Oh, Glory to the Cleansing Blood	12
I cannot See the Way	51	ONWARD, SOLDIERS	5
I CALLED UPON THE LORD	53	Oh, Wondrously Sweet is the Story	18
I SHALL GO HOME SOME DAY	40	OUR GLORIOUS HOME	37
I AM COMING TO THEE	134	Oh, the Precious Word of Jesus	26
I AM SO GLAD	55	OH, FOR A FAITH	54
I am Rejoicing Day by Day	55	One by One the Loving Master	129
I'M ON MY JOURNEY HOME	146	ON CHRIST ALONE I LEAN	126
I AM ETERNALLY FREE	76	ON TO THE FRONT	131
I DO BELIEVE	69	ONWARD FOREVER	119
In the Day of all Days	175	Oh, What can Little Hands Do?	120
IN SACRED LAYS	180	ONWARD, HOMEWARD	93
I Will Sing the Praise of Jesus	145	ONLY WAIT	89
		OH, BE JOYFUL	80
Just as I am, Without one Plea	11	OVER THE BORDER-LAND	77
Jesus, When He left the Sky	21	OH, WORSHIP THE KING	73
JESUS LOVES ME	43	O BETHLEHEM	70
JESUS IS CALLING	139	ONWARD, CHRISTIAN SOLDIERS	35
JUNIOR LEAGUE CHORUS	125	O WAND'RER FROM THE FOLD	184
JESUS IS CALLING TO THEE	102	OH, FOR A HEART TO PRAISE	176
JUST THE SAME TO-DAY	171	ONWARD, BE OUR WATCHWORD	117
LET IT FALL ON ME	169	PROTECTING ROCK	7
LITTLE ONES LIKE ME	21	PALACE IN THE VALE	129
LET ME GO TO JESUS	30	PRAISES TO OUR KING	118
Like the Sound of Many Waters	34	PLACE I LOVE, (The)	163
LET ME CLING, O ROCK OF AGES	36	PUBLISH THE MESSAGE	68
Listen, O Listen, I've Something	43	PRECIOUS LOVE OF JESUS	59
LITTLE STARS FOR JESUS	49	PASSING AWAY	182
Letting Jesus Lead	132		
Light-House by the Sea, (The)	38	Quit the Paths of Sin and Folly	132
Lo! a Gleam from Yonder	160		
LAMBS OF THE FLOCK	128	Rock of Ages, Shelter Me	7
LIFT THE CROSS OF JESUS	161	RING OUT SALVATION'S SOUND	16
LET THE GOSPEL SHINE	164	ROCK OF AGES	44
LORD'S PRAYER, (The)	100	RIPE IS THE GRAIN	133
LEAD KINDLY LIGHT	84	RAISE THE SIGNAL	121
LORD IS MY SHEPHERD, (The) No. 1	142	REAPER AND THE FLOWERS	157
Let Me In	178	RESPONSIVE READINGS	174, 165, 186, 188, 103
LEAD ME, FATHER	167	RALLYING SONG	86
My Country, 'Tis of Thee	10		
My Hope is Built on Nothing Less	47	SWEET IS THE STORY	18
MORNING HYMN	136	SAVIOR, PILOT ME	50
MARCHING TO GLORY	104	Serene I Laid Me Down	140
MUST JESUS BEAR THE CROSS	98	SUNDAY-SCHOOL ARMY	153
MARCHING ON	91	See the Mighty Host Advancing	104
MORE LIKE JESUS	67	SONG OF PRAISE, (A)	103
MY SHEPHERD LEADS	63	SOME DAY WE'LL MEET	97
MY SONG SHALL BE OF JESUS	177	SOME SWEET DAY	14

INDEX

Title	No.	Title	No.
Shout, O Earth	95	The Lord is My Shepherd. No. 1.	142
Satisfied with Jesus	87	The Banner of the Cross	29
Singing with the Angels	82		
Story of the Christ	71	Unto Him I'll Go	19
Shall I be Worthy	179	Unto Thee Will I Sing	137
Scatter the Seed	23	Under His Banner	181
Soldiers of the Lord	170		
		Who will Accept Him	4
There is Sunshine and Love	6	We are Waiting at the Cross	13
The Protecting Rock	7	With a Song and a Prayer	2
The Way of the Lord is Best	3	Won't You Try, My Brother?	3
There are Angels Hovering Ever	15	Welcome the Angels In	15
There is Work for You and Me	25	Wonderful News	20
The Fields Lay Whitening	33	We are Pilgrims to a Home	22
Thank and Praise Him	41	When the Mists have Cleared	24
The Lord is My Shepherd, No. 2.	150	We are Little Pilgrims	45
The Lord is My Refuge	147	When the Last Farewell is Spoken	48
The World for Christ	124	We'll Overthrow the Wrong	143
There is a Reaper Whose Name is	157	We are Soldiers of a Mighty Army	143
There is a Land, a Sunny Land	156	We are Marching On	123
The Golden Somewhere	155	We are Little Toilers	149
The Sunday-School Army	153	Working for the Master	127
The Bells of Time	110	We are Children of a King	106
The Door of the Kingdom	107	We Thank Thee, Father	116
The Children's Hymn	122	What His Little Ones can Do	115
The Coming of the King	112	We can Scatter as We Go	115
The Crowning By and By	111	Why Stand Ye Here Idle?	168
To Please the King	120	White as Snow	99
The Place I Love	163	When the Great Day Comes	94
The Lord's Prayer	100	Wake the World	66
The Wondrous Man	92	When We Reach the Harbor	62
Thankful Be	75	With Thankful Acclaim	173
To Him that Overcometh	72		
Trusting in Jesus	64	Your Lamb or Mine	158
Toiling in Life's Harvest	57	Yes, We'll Praise Him	81

SONGS FOR PRIMARY AND INFANT CLASSES.

Title	No.	Title	No.
A Little Child	31	Lambs of the Flock	128
Child's Evening Prayer	65	Rallying Song	86
Children's Day	52, 108	Sunday School Army	153
Children's Hymn	122	Story of the Christ	71
God Bless the Little Ones	130	To Please the King	120
God is Love	101	The Lord's Prayer	100
Happy as We Labor	42	The Wondrous Man	92
I Do Believe	69	We are Little Pilgrims	45
Little Ones Like Me	21	What His Little Ones can Do	115
Little Stars for Jesus	49		

SUITABLE FOR FUNERALS.

Title	No.	Title	No.
By and by will Come the Morning	154	Lead, Kindly Light	84
Doubt Not God's Good Purpose	138	On Christ Alone I Lean	126
From Earth to Heaven	48	The Palace in the Vale	129
God Knows	51	Reaper and the Flowers	157
He Leadeth Me	96	Some Sweet Day	14
I shall Go Home Some Day	40	When the Mists have Cleared	24
Let Me Cling, O Rock of Ages	36	When the Great Day Comes	94

www.ingramcontent.com/pod-product-compliance
Lightning Source LLC
Chambersburg PA
CBHW020903230426
43666CB00008B/1288